Travel in the
TWENTIES
and
THIRTIES

INTRODUCTION

The interwar years did not see a return to the prosperity of the Edwardian era: the 1920s saw a self conscious examination of the foundation and presumptions of western society together with a somewhat hedonistic quest for oblivious happiness; a crisis of confidence amongst politicians and intellectuals and the creation of the epithet 'gay twenties' to describe the antics of the bright young people, as depicted in the novels of Aldous Huxley. In the 1930s, the economic depression and the worsening political situation in Europe made it impossible to bury one's head in the sand, reflected by the serious and earnest nature of debate at the Oxford Union and the way thousands voluntarily fought in the International Brigades during the Spanish Civil War — a response which had not been witnessed since the help given to the Greeks in their fight for independence from Turkey in 1823. Yet against this rather gloomy background, these years were in many ways something of a 'golden age' for travellers. They were years of great excitement for manufacturers of transport hardware and public alike. Public transport was not subject to the drastic cuts following World War II, and bus services in particular were improved so that rural areas enjoyed unprecedented mobility. At the same time, personalised transport in the form of the motor car and motor bike gave an independence which not even the aristocracy had enjoyed before World War I.

Travel over any distance had automatically meant the use of the railway and the aristocrats who had a private carriage to attach to public trains, such as the Duke of Sutherland, were within single figures. Even that privilege conferred a very limited independence. Edward VII could remark in 1895 that 'we are all socialists now' — not such a silly remark as many Fabians must have thought it — and the French coined the phrase the democratisation of travel. Facilitating the spread of ideas and news, it was the railways which had brought this about so that for Duke and commoner alike, travel implied an absence of privacy — the most one could expect or hope for was a compartment to oneself. It was an end to this state of affairs that was perhaps the most

Below: Gatwick airport opened to air traffic on 9 December 1931 with a flight to Le Bourget but the official opening by Viscount Swinton was not until 6 June 1932. Here a Fokker airliner waits to leave. *Radio Times Hulton Picture Library*

Travel in the
TWENTIES
and
THIRTIES

Travel in the TWENTIES and THIRTIES

Anthony J. Lambert

LONDON

IAN ALLAN LTD

First published 1983

ISBN 0 7110 1051 X

© Anthony J. Lambert 1983

Published by Ian Allan Ltd, Shepperton, Surrey;
and printed by Ian Allan Printing Ltd at their
works at Coombelands in Runnymede, England

Previous page: The Cunard liner *Scythia*
(21,500tons) leaving Barrow in 1921 after
fitting out there. She was launched on
23 March 1920.   *R. Sankey*

Acknowledgements
For their kind assistance in the preparation of
this book, the author wishes to acknowledge
his gratitude to the following: Messrs
T. W. Baker-Jones, W. Boddy, D. C. Brech,
W. A. Camwell, T. J. Edgington, D. Johnson,
J. Joyce, S. Mills, G. A. Oliver, S. Rabson,
S. Rhodes, Mrs V. M. Russell, Messrs
R. Sankey, P. K. Wilkinson, P. Wilson,
L. A. Winter; and to the various organisations
for their kind permission to reproduce
photographs.

CONTENTS

enduring and potentially harmful change wrought by the interwar years. Harmful because the western world has come to regard personal transport in the form of a car as a right, while the means of sustaining it diminish at an alarming rate.

But such gloomy thoughts did not trouble the pioneers of the people's car to whom the prospect of individual mobility meant good profits, although there were as many bankruptcies as profitable firms in the twenties. For the growing numbers who could afford a car, it meant an end to the tyranny of the timetable and a new concept of freedom. Oil was a seemingly inexhaustible commodity and no one asked how much there was, any more than one would have expected the early railway promoters to inquire about our coal reserves.

The railways, of course, suffered a loss of revenue, both from falling passenger revenue on relatively short journeys, and from the gradual loss of freight traffic, largely caused by the huge number of redundant army lorry chassis for sale after the war being adapted for commercial use. But the railways fought hard to retain traffic and few branch lines were closed. So during the interwar years, a good balance between public and private transport existed. The railways had to campaign for a 'square deal' from the government vis-a-vis taxation and restrictive legislation, something they have yet to be given, but the customer had the best of both worlds — a good public transport service by train, bus and tram, and the opportunity for personal mobility on reasonably traffic-free roads.

Perhaps the outstanding factor which characterised all forms of travel during these years was the quest for speed. The age was obsessed with record breaking, whether it be competition for the Blue Riband on the North Atlantic, the Schneider trophy, the intense competition between the London, Midland & Scottish Railway and the London & North Eastern Railway over the London to Scotland services and the world speed record for a steam engine, or what could be achieved with an internal combustion engine on land. Some idea of the importance attached to 'first time' transport events and new records can be gained by the scale of reception given to Lindbergh in New York after his solo flight across the Atlantic, pictured in this book. We are still dedicated to cutting journey times but the means by which we do it is rarely a cause for great excitement. The advent and sophistication of the High Speed Train is admired but it now takes the presence of a steam engine to pack the platforms at Paddington; even the elegance and technical excellence of Concorde has been over-shadowed by the debate regarding its utility.

Civil aviation was in its infancy during the interwar years and the teething problems were well on their way to resolution by 1939. But during those years, its development affected the business and diplomatic communities rather than the public. The high number of accidents and general unreliability of early services did not encourage acceptance of the speed advantage as sufficient reason to forsake rail travel, particularly when the benefit was marginal.

Comforts were by no means lacking on many flights by 1939. Much the same kind of services were provided on interwar flights as today — even movies were being screened. Many routes were established to serve far-flung outposts of the Empire and facilitate diplomatic communication.

So the steamship companies were hardly affected by the airlines and the era saw the commissioning of perhaps the finest liners that will ever be built. Liners were regarded not only as floating hotels reflecting the standing of their owners (and passengers), but also as ambassadors of their country and as such governments were willing to subsidise their construction. While the design of railway carriages never returned to the heavy elegance of the Victorian and Edwardian years, the grandeur and sophistication of passenger liners reached an apogee. The trans-Atlantic crossing was the most fashionable journey of the time, outshining the Blue Train, the Orient Express and certainly any of the sea routes to the Orient. The maiden voyage of one of the great liners saw a gathering of 'high society' embracing politicians, aristocrats, wealthy industrialists and the more affluent writers. Newspapers would describe them and their first journey in detail and the banks of the Solent would be crowded if Southampton was the destination.

Holidays became more of a norm although it is remarkable how many people never left their home town from one year's end to the next, even by 1939. There were excursions in plenty, many organised by employers as a day out for their employees, but the package holiday had yet to afflict such places as Torremelinos and the Costa del Sol. The motor car syphoned off some holiday traffic from the railways and traffic jams became one of the less appealing aspects of summer. Nonetheless, the number of excursion trains run on summer Saturdays was prodigious, causing headaches for operating departments and delight for railway photographers who would gather at classic locations like Dawlish or Dainton to capture the seemingly endless procession of packed trains.

Below: It was natural for the village blacksmith to adapt his business to cater for the motor car. His livelihood was threatened by the diminishing number of horses to shoe, caused not only by the motor car and lorry but also the gradual mechanisation of agriculture. Inevitably many blacksmiths continued their customary trade long after installing petrol pumps. This view of a garage at Walkerburn, Peebleshire in 1937 shows a Morris Eight. *D. C. Thomson & Co Ltd*

The advertising industry boom is a post-World War II phenomenon but transport was perhaps the first industry to exploit the potential of the hoarding. Hardly surprising when the railways in particular had such a large captive audience. The enamel signs familiar to today's railway museum visitors had lent a colourful note to Victorian stations, but between the wars these mushroomed in size, number and concept. Nor were the railways slow to realise the benefits of advertising on their own behalf. London Transport set high standards for itself in a commendably good series of posters before World War I, and the Great Western Railway developed a remarkably sophisticated publicity department producing such disparate items as jigsaws of its crack trains amidst attractive scenery and illustrated books marketing the delightful suburban properties that could be bought near its stations. Poster design for railway companies attained the status of art with the work of men like Cassandre, McKnight Kauffer and Wilkinson in Europe and Ben Shahn in America.

Travel in the
TWENTIES
and
THIRTIES

RAIL TRAVEL

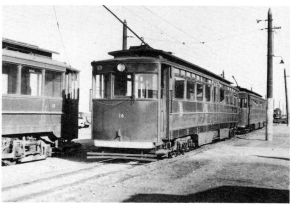

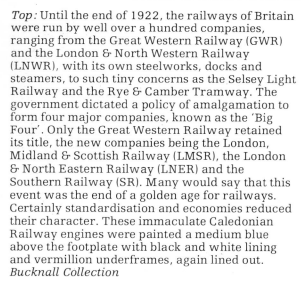

Top: Until the end of 1922, the railways of Britain were run by well over a hundred companies, ranging from the Great Western Railway (GWR) and the London & North Western Railway (LNWR), with its own steelworks, docks and steamers, to such tiny concerns as the Selsey Light Railway and the Rye & Camber Tramway. The government dictated a policy of amalgamation to form four major companies, known as the 'Big Four'. Only the Great Western Railway retained its title, the new companies being the London, Midland & Scottish Railway (LMSR), the London & North Eastern Railway (LNER) and the Southern Railway (SR). Many would say that this event was the end of a golden age for railways. Certainly standardisation and economies reduced their character. These immaculate Caledonian Railway engines were painted a medium blue above the footplate with black and white lining and vermillion underframes, again lined out.
Bucknall Collection

Above: Of the four major railway companies, only the Southern Railway adopted electric traction on a large scale. There were, however, a few isolated experiments by the other companies and such a line was the Grimsby and Immingham Electric Railway which the LNER inherited from the Great Central Railway in 1922. The GCR built the line in 1912 to serve the new docks at Immingham. A

half-hourly service was provided by two cars which met at No 8 Passing Place, operating day and night. Supplementary trains were run in accordance with shift workings at the docks and factories. Until 1942, the cars were finished in LNER varnished teak or dark brown.   *D. Tate*

Above: Throughout the 1920s and 1930s, the railways retained their position as the prime carriers of the nation's goods. Long-distance lorries were still a thing of the future and it was generally only on short-distance hauls that the commercial vehicle had made serious inroads in the railways' business. Here GWR 2-6-0 No 4331 is seen heading a typical mixed freight train including general merchandise vans, private-owner coal wagons and a cattle van.
Bucknall Collection

Right: The Metropolitan Railway was a much more extensive concern than the present Metropolitan underground line would suggest. Its furthermost point was Verney Junction in the heart of Buckinghamshire, beyond Aylesbury. A northbound main line fast train hauled by No 20 before it received a name passes West Hampstead. The third coach is one of the two Pullman buffet cars which apppeared in 1910, enabling bar-proppers to continue drinking on the midnight train from Baker Street.   *London Transport*

Above: The locomotive *Flying Scotsman* was built in 1922 to the designs of Sir Nigel Gresley — who became chief mechanical engineer on the LNER at the Grouping — and entered service on expresses to Edinburgh and Leeds in the following year. It is unlikely that this engine would have captured the imagination of the public had a train not been given the same name in 1862. In 1928 the 'Flying Scotsman' was turned into a non-stop service from Kings Cross to Edinburgh, leaving at the traditional time of 10.0am. A corridor was provided through the tender to enable the engine crew to be relieved at the half way point. Most of Gresley's A3 class were named after racehorses and here No 2795 *Call Boy* is seen passing Langley with the down 'Flying Scotsman' in 1933.
Real Photographs

Above right: With the growth of bus commuting, the opportunities open to the railways to develop local traffic were limited. Many halts were opened on branch lines to reduce journey times to the local station but it was generally a rearguard action. A rare exception was the development of an industrial estate or factory creating a need for a station. On 22 September 1938, a new station was opened at Apsley, Hertfordshire on the Watford to Hemel Hempstead line to cater for the 5,000 employees at the paper factory of John Dickinson & Co. The train is breaking a paper hoop before the opening ceremony by Lord Stamp, chairman of the LMS, and Sir Reginald Bonson, chairman of Dickinson's. Note the newsreel cameraman on the left. *Radio Times Hulton Picture Library*

Right: An August morning in 1934 at Kings Cross with the holiday rush in full spate. On the right is the 'Flying Scotsman' and the express to its left is probably a relief working or bound for a resort such as Scarborough. The growth of holiday camps, like Filey, near Scarborough, enabled many more to take a holiday than would have done so before World War I. Yet as late as 1939 less than half the population left home even for a single night in the year.
Radio Times Hulton Picture Library

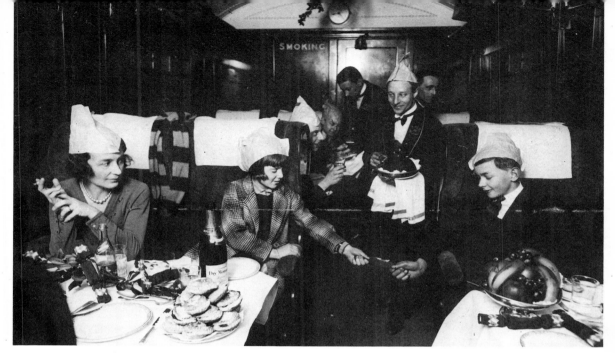

Top left: Gresley's 'P2' class was a precursor to the 'A4' class of which *Mallard* was the most famous. They were the only eight-coupled express locomotives to run in this country and were specifically designed for express work in Scotland where the small diameter driving wheel and large cylinders made them ideal on hilly routes. In designing them, Gresley borrowed from the French locomotive designer Chapelon, and *Cock o' the North* even went over to the Vitry experimental station near Paris for tests. Here No 2001 *Cock o' the North* is seen at Kings Cross. *F. R. Hebron*

Centre left: For many years, the world's fastest regular steam train was the GWR's 'Cheltenham Flyer', seen here speeding through Pangbourne in June 1932. When the 2.30pm from Paddington to Cheltenham was accelerated for the 1923 timetable, an average speed of 61.8mph was required for the stretch to Swindon. By 1932, the usual engine was a 'Castle' class 4-6-0 and averages of 81mph for the 77 miles from London to Swindon were customary.
Radio Times Hulton Picture Library

Bottom left: A GWR 'Star' class heads west past Dawlish Warren with the 'Cornish Riviera Express' in August 1939. When the first regular non-stop service between Paddington and Plymouth was inaugurated on 1 July 1904, it was the world's longest daily non-stop run. The train represented the classic example of slip coach and through carriage working, shedding coaches at intervals along its journey to Plymouth and carrying through carriages for the Cornish resorts of Newquay, Falmouth and St Ives.

Above: For Christmas 1931, the LNER publicised their 'Flying Scotsman' service by arranging for the customary Christmas trimmings to be available on the train. Mince pies, Christmas pudding, crackers, champagne and fruit bowl are evident. Note the 'Smoking' sign — a survival of the earliest days of railway travel when the smoker had to find a compartment to indulge his habit. *Radio Times Hulton Picture Library*

Left: A stocking and presents beside a sleeping girl on the 'Flying Scotsman' in December 1931. Quite how the absence of a chimney for Santa Claus to enter was explained to the child has not been recorded. The crackers on her right are named 'Bang Full Delight Crackers', a trade name which would probably guarantee minimal sales in our more critical age.
Radio Times Hulton Picture Library

Below: LNER 'A4' Pacific *Silver Link*. On 27 September 1935, *Silver Link* took part in a demonstration run for the press and guests of the company to see what could be achieved between London and Grantham. Few expected the engine to achieve 112mph or to complete 81 miles in the first hour. The 'Silver Jubilee' express entered regular service on the following Monday and it is interesting to note that speed recorders were fitted in the cabs of the engine so that the Running Superintendent could check that no speed restrictions were broken. *Real Photographs*

Bottom: Every schoolboy knows *Mallard* as the engine which holds the world speed record for steam of 126mph, achieved during a special trial on Sunday 3 July 1938. Three years before, a sister engine *Silver Link* had managed 112mph during a demonstration of the Silver Jubilee streamlined express between Kings Cross and Grantham. The entire train was painted silver and it began its daily service between Newcastle and London in September 1935. Here *Mallard* nears Potters Bar with a down Leeds express.
Real Photographs

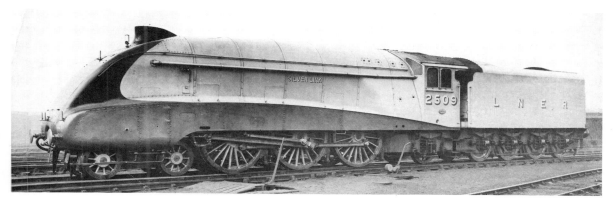

Right : For the Coronation year, the LNER introduced a six-hour service to Edinburgh with an entirely new train, weighing almost half as much again as the 'Silver Jubilee'. A trial run from Kings Cross to Grantham took place on 30 June 1937, the day after the LMS had taken the world speed record for steam from the LNER by reaching 114mph. Much as the LNER would have liked to regain the honour, the run down Stoke bank to Peterborough did not see more than 109mph reached. This photograph was taken during the trial run.
Radio Times Hulton Picture Library

Left: The 'Coronation' incorporated an elegant, streamlined beaver-tail observation car from which this view was taken during the trial run on 30 June 1937. The goods train is waiting in an adjacent loop. The locomotives for the train were painted in the usual garter blue but the coaches were finished in garter blue to the waistline and upper panels in Cambridge blue.
Radio Times Hulton Picture Library

Left: The 'Coronation Scot' was introduced by the LMS to celebrate the Coronation of King George VI in 1937. Following a remarkable series of successful tests in 1936, it was anticipated that the train would be allowed six hours for the 401 miles from London to Glasgow. In the event the management opted for a cautious $6\frac{1}{2}$ hours. The engines and coaches were specially built and finished in royal blue with white stripes. It was the period when the LMS and LNER were in fierce competition to secure the world speed record for a steam engine and in June 1937 a speed of 114mph was attained by the Coronation Scot. The engine *Coronation* No 6220 was sent to America in 1939 for the New York World's Fair and made an extensive tour, visiting Washington, Pittsburgh, St. Louis, Chicago, Detroit, and Boston before reaching New York. No 6221 *Queen Elizabeth* is seen here climbing to Shap Summit.
Radio Times Hulton Picture Library

Below: The 'Coronation Scot' leaving Euston for Glasgow in July 1937. It is thought that the streamlining of the LMS Pacifics was probably more effective in reducing air resistance than that of the LNER. The LMS made a splendid film entitled *Coronation Scot* which has captured the grace of a streamlined engine hard at work. Surprisingly the LNER did not record their achievements on film.
Radio Times Hulton Picture Library

Left: Some idea of the excitement caused by the rivalry between the LMS and LNER for a new world speed record for steam is given by this crowd greeting Driver James Clarke on his return to Euston on 17 November 1936. On the previous day he had bettered the target of six hours for the 401.4-mile non-stop journey to Glasgow and completed the return journey in 344 minutes at an average speed of 70mph. The maximum speed attained was only 95mph but the following year was to see dramatic changes with the introduction of the streamlined 'Coronation Scot'. *Radio Times Hulton Picture Library*

Below: Like the 'Flying Scotsman', the name 'Royal Scot' was given to an engine as well as a train. Unlike the 'Flying Scotsman' however, the engine came first in 1927 although the train also began in the summer of that year. Only two stops were made on its journey from Euston to Glasgow, at Carnforth to change engines and at Symington where the Glasgow and Edinburgh portions were divided. During the following winter, it ran non-stop to Carlisle. For the 1928 service, new coaches were provided for the LMS travelling hotel, as they called it, incorporating a boudoir, lounge and bar. Private dining rooms were provided and the coaches were decorated in differing styles — Jacobean, Chippendale, etc. This view of the lounge was taken in July 1928. *Radio Times Hulton Picture Library*

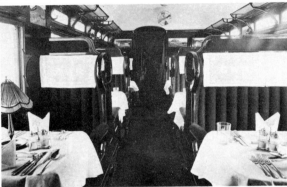

Top: Sir Josiah Stamp, seated on the left, trying the new buffet carriage of the LMS on 2 June 1932. The coaches were an innovation for the LMS, providing a cafeteria with barmaids. Sir Josiah Stamp (1880-1941) was Chairman of the LMS and was made a peer in 1938 until his premature death in an air-raid.
Radio Times Hulton Picture Library

Above & right: Of the four pre-nationalisation railway companies, the GWR had the most progressive and enterprising publicity and advertising department. All kinds of ideas were exploited to keep the name of the GWR to the fore, from jig-saw puzzles and painting books for children to sophisticated advertising campaigns and a wide range of books to introduce potential travellers of the attractions which could be visited by the railway. Part of the department's work was to record the railways' work and facilities on film for use in publicity material. The interior of the first class dining car of the Great Western's articulated passenger train of 1925 is here compared with a third class car from the LNER 'Coronation' of twelve years later. The solidly traditional changed swiftly during the 1930s and in the 1937 train there are traces of 'art deco' in the decoration and light fittings.
Ian Allan Library

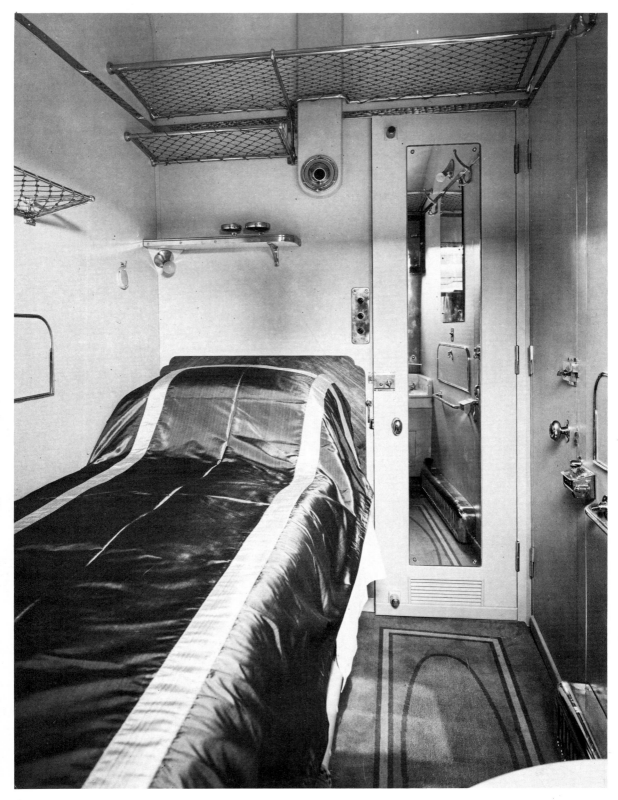

Left: The sleeping car, or bed-carriages as they were initially called, is almost as old as the railway, the first appearing in 1838 on the London & Birmingham and Grand Junction Railways between London and Lancashire. On the GWR they remained an exclusively first-class amenity until 1928, when they were offered to 3rd class passengers although no linen was provided, only a pillow and blanket. This compartment was typical of the best that the LMS offered in 1935 and compared favourably to a good hotel. *Ian Allan Library*

Right & above: It seems unlikely that the Buffet car would have been approved of by Edwardian travellers. To have had to perch on stools at a bar would not have been many first class passengers' idea of eating or drinking in a civilised manner. But of course the Dining car was only phased out on certain trains by the new type of carriages which were probably intended for the slightly less affluent. They economised on staff and the time needed to serve light refreshments. This interior of a GWR Buffet car was taken in July 1934. By contrast, this is the art deco interior of an SR buffet car built for Bognor line electric services at about the same time. *Ian Allan Library*

Above left: A day at the races — racegoers at Waterloo preparing to leave for Ascot on 19 June 1934. Pullman trains were often arranged for the wealthier followers of the turf and there was certainly no stigma attached to arriving by public transport. One wonders what proportion travels by train today.
Radio Times Hulton Picture Library

Left: Tattenham Corner station on Derby Day in May 1922. Race meetings called for a large number of special workings, not only to convey spectators but the horses, jockeys, stable lads and tack from their stables. The rows of horse boxes on the right of the picture indicate the importance of this traffic. Hunt meetings and travelling circuses were also dependent upon the railways. In the latter case, entire trains were permanently at the disposal of the circus during its tour.
Radio Times Hulton Picture Library

Above: The scene at Victoria station at the beginning of the state visit of King Leopold III of the Belgians on 16 November 1937. King Leopold is talking to King George VI on the right. His great-uncle King Leopold II of the Belgians had been a patron of international train travel, lending his name to the list of subscribing shareholders of Nagelmackers' 'Companie Internationale des Wagon-Lits et des Grands Express Europeens' which pioneered the concept of luxury international train travel in Europe.
Radio Times Hulton Picture Library

Top: An ex-London & South Western Railway Class T9 No 338 waits to leave the specially constructed station at Airways House, the new Imperial Airways headquarters at Victoria, on 6 June 1939. It was the first train to leave from the new station to convey passengers to Southampton Docks for the Empire Flying Boat Services. *Radio Times Hulton Picture Library*

Above: On 27 May 1936, the Cunard White Star Liner *Queen Mary* left Southampton on her maiden voyage to New York. A special Pullman train conveying passengers for embarkation is seen here arriving at the quayside in Southampton. The engine is appropriately one of the 'Lord Nelson' class No 852 *Sir Walter Raleigh*. *Radio Times Hulton Picture Library*

Above: The 'King' class was the apogee of express passenger design on the Great Western Railway, if not the final one. Introduced in 1927 the first of the class No 6000 *King George V* was requested by the Baltimore & Ohio Railway to represent Britain at their centenary celebrations. The clean lines of the engine made a favourable impression and as railways originated in England, *King George V* was given pride of place at the head of the procession of locomotives at Halethorpe, USA. After the exhibition, she hauled a special train from Baltimore to Washington and Philadelphia and back. *King George V* has been preserved and is in the custody of Bulmer's at Hereford.   *LPC*

Below: No station in London had a more grandiose approach than the old Euston. Philip Hardwick's elegant but simple Doric Portico was a perfect introduction to his later great hall beyond, the frieze to the ornate and magnificent ceiling decorated with allegorical panels of the principal towns on the LNWR. When built, the columns of the arch were higher than those of any other building in London at the time. In a classic instance of official vandalism, it was demolished in 1967 to make way for the anonymous glass and concrete box which now defaces the site of the old station. In this view of 1925, taxis wait for custom.   *LPC*

Below: On 13 September 1926, the 'Golden Arrow Express' began running between Calais and Paris. The train was specially built and was considered the last word in modern comfort. It is seen here entering Calais Maritime behind a Nord Pacific. The practice of carrying the carriages across the Channel did not begin until October 1936. *Popperfoto*

Right: English railway companies may have been justly proud of the facilities and standard of comfort on their named expresses but they diminish in stature in comparison with those across the Atlantic. The Florida Special was one of the fastest long distance trains, covering the 1,388 miles from New York to Miami in 27hrs 45mins. The Florida East Coast Railway provided the services of a hostess, an orchestra, a full-sized recreation car and facilities for dancing and bridge. This picture also shows the emergence of more personalised transport — the tiny single seater aeroplane known as the 'Flying Flea'. *Popperfoto*

Bottom right: The way we travel and the reasons for it have and continue to change. Perhaps the only constants are the joy or sadness felt on station platforms and in airport terminals as relatives and friends meet or part, or the anticipation engendered on a train to a sporting occasion. Here crowds climb off a Shepperton line train at Kempton Park for the races. *Ian Allan Library*

Bottom far right: The Southwold Railway, opened in 1879 to 3ft gauge and running from Halesworth on the Great Eastern Railway main line, was once a busy and quite prosperous concern — for a rural branch line. In 1900, over 100,000 passengers and 15,000 tons of freight were carried. It was a flat, easy line to work, the only major engineering feature being a swing bridge over the river Blyth. Bus competition hit traffic returns seriously, so much so that in April 1929, the London management gave a week's notice to the employees and the locals that the line would close. Doubtless people who had never supported the line turned out to witness the closure. Even Pathé News sent a camera crew to cover what was then a rare event — the closure of a railway. This is the scene at Southwold on the final day. *Suffolk Photographic Survey*

Below: The engine-driver and fireman were once revered figures, representing the aspirations of many a child who waved at the two exposed men as a matter of course. There was something very special about seeing a steam engine after dark with the light from the firebox silhouetting the shovelling fireman and the driver peering into the night for signal lamps. Now they are hardly visible. A driver and fireman carrying billy cans and lunch boxes knock off at Holbeck Shed, Leeds. *Popperfoto*

AIR TRAVEL

Above: Airship R80 at Barrow. At a conference held in February 1920 under the Chairmanship of Air Commodore Maitland to consider passenger accommodation and other requirements for commercial rigid airships, it was recommended that owing to the small size of R80, it would be more usefully employed on day rather than overnight flights. The conference met at a time when civil aviation was in its infancy, the world's first daily air service and the first international scheduled flight having begun in the previous year. The conference unanimously recommended that a car built into the hull was superior to a slung car since it was more spacious and offered less resistance. R33 R36, and R37 should be fitted with cars containing sleeping accommodation. As much cooked food as possible should always be carried so that the necessity for cooking food would be reduced to a minimum. Heat for cooking and warming should be provided by steam generated from exhaust gases with auxillary paraffin heating. Windows of cars should not be made to open. Water should be provided for washing but not for lavatories so no septic tanks were required. Electric light was considered essential. *R. Sankey*

Below: Although six months before the 1920s began, the epic flight of R34 across the Atlantic deserves inclusion. On 2 July 1919, the R34 set out with a crew of 31 from East Fortune on the coast of Scotland and flew to New York in 108 hours and accomplished the return journey in 75 hours. Based on the design of the captured Zeppelin L33, the R34 was fitted with five 275hp Sunbeam engines and had a capacity of two million cubic feet. The airship was completely destroyed in June 1921, the forepart being battered against the ground when anchored in the open. The R34 is seen here at Mineola USA after the first crossing.
Radio Times Hulton Picture Library

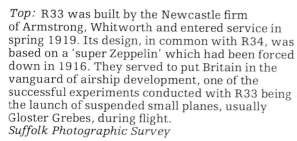

Top: R33 was built by the Newcastle firm of Armstrong, Whitworth and entered service in spring 1919. Its design, in common with R34, was based on a 'super Zeppelin' which had been forced down in 1916. They served to put Britain in the vanguard of airship development, one of the successful experiments conducted with R33 being the launch of suspended small planes, usually Gloster Grebes, during flight.
Suffolk Photographic Survey

Above left: In 1924 a contract was placed by the British Government with the Airship Guarantee Company of Howden for the construction of two giant airships with a capacity of over five million cubic feet. The R101 was larger than the R100 and at the time of the maiden flight in autumn 1930, R101 was the largest airship in the world. Accommodation was arranged on two decks, the upper containing a lounge, dining-room for 50 and

cabins, and on the lower were a smoking room, electric kitchens, crew's quarters and additional cabins. Initial tests had only been carried out in good quiet weather when officials gave permission for her first commercial flight. On the gusty evening of 4 October 1930, R101 left Cardington, Bedfordshire for India. At 1,000 feet, the airship rolled and pitched heavily and the Channel was crossed at a low altitude. Soon after 2.0am R101 was near Beauvais, north of Paris, when air currents sent her into a nose dive which ended in disaster. The ship was soon a mass of flames and 48 of the 54 passengers died, including the Air Minister. The R101 is seen here at Cardington in June 1930.
Suffolk Photographic Survey

Above right: The control cabin of R33, photographed at Pulham St Mary, near Diss in Norfolk, in 1926. *Suffolk Photographic Survey*

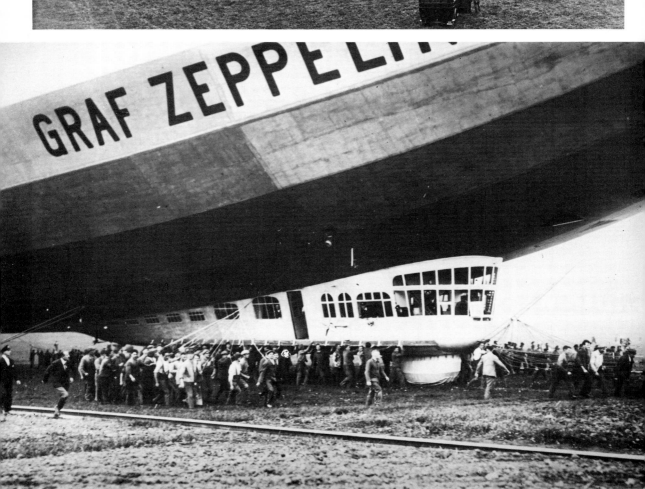

Above left: Count von Zeppelin (1838-1917), a retired German army officer, designer of the first successful rigid framed airship. He launched his first airship, the LZ1 on 2 July 1900 and the 420ft long dirigible flew for an hour and a quarter over Lake Constance, attaining with her two 16hp Daimler engines a maximum speed of 20mph, but crashed on landing. Zeppelin's contribution to airship development was acknowledged by subsequent airships bearing his name. The most famous Zeppelin was the *Graf Zeppelin* which was begun in 1927. Its capacity was over $3\frac{1}{2}$ million cubic feet and the length 772ft. Accommodation included a saloon, a dining room, and ten double berth sleeping compartments. In August 1931, the LZ 127 visited England, seen here landing at Hanworth Park, Middlesex with a load of German tourists. Twenty-four British passengers then embarked for a 24-hour cruise around England. *Popperfoto*

Left: The *Graf Zeppelin* was the first commercial airship to cross the Atlantic, on 11 October 1928 flying from Friedrichshaven, base of the state-owned German Zeppelin Transport Company, to Lakehurst in New Jersey. In the following year, the LZ 127 circumnavigated the earth, completing the 21,300 miles in 21 days. In 1932, a regular mail and passenger service was inaugurated between Friedrichshaven and Rio de Janeiro by the *Graf Zeppelin*. There were no trans-Atlantic plane services at that time and passengers would connect with the airship service by train or shorter journey aeroplanes. From Rio, aeroplane connections were advertised on to Porto Alegre, Montevideo, Buenos Aires and Santiago de Chile. The baggage allowance was 286lb although 220lb was carried by German steamships free of extra charge. This view shows the airship being manhandled to the ground in 1930. In March 1940, the Graf Zeppelin was broken up to provide metal for additions to the Luftwaffe, despite pleas that the ship should be preserved as a museum piece. *Radio Times Hulton Picture Library*

Above: Named after the Prussian soldier and statesman who invited Hitler to assume the Chancellorship of Germany in 1933, the *Hindenburg* was the largest airship ever built. Completed in March 1936, the *Hindenburg* had a gas capacity of over seven million cubic feet. The 25 staterooms were fitted with hot and cold water and the upper deck also held the dining room, lounge, reading and writing rooms and two promenades. The lower deck contained the kitchens, smoking-room, bathrooms and crew's quarters. In the following year, on 6 May 1937, the *Hindenburg* erupted in flames while docking at Lakehurst, New Jersey. Thirty-five of the 97 people on board died. To a generation accustomed to few survivors from aeroplane crashes, it is remarkable that anyone emerged alive from such a holocaust. The Board of Inquiry attributed the cause to a combination of the atmospheric conditions created by a thunderstorm and escaping hydrogen from one of the cells. Suggestions of sabotage against the swastika-emblazoned ship have never been completely disproved. *Popperfoto*

Left: The Short Calcutta was an important advance in flying-boat design, being the first for commercial service to have a stressed skin metal hull. Fifteen passengers were carried, served by a steward with hot or cold meals from a buffet. G-EBVG was the first of the two aircraft ordered by Imperial Airways and it is seen here on the Thames at Westminster, after landing on 1 August 1928 for a three day visit to enable an inspection by members of Parliament. The Calcuttas were ordered for the Genoa to Alexandria section of the Karachi service. Passengers flew by A. W. Argosy from Croydon to Basle where a sleeping car express was taken for Genoa. A DH66 Hercules handled the final leg from Alexandria to Karachi. *British Airways*

Below: The huge German Dornier DO-X on Lake Constance (Boden See) prior to its successful crossing of the Atlantic in 1931. Having twelve engines and a wing span of 148ft, the design of the fuselage owed more to nautical ideas than most flying boats. *Flight International*

Bottom: Short Kent class flying boat G-ABFC *Satyrus*. These came into service in 1931 on the Brindisi to Alexandria run, carrying 16 passengers besides mail. *Satyrus* was the last of three Kents to be delivered to Imperial Airways and received extensive publicity by carrying HRH The Prince of Wales on a tour of the Solent area in May 1931. The Kents were a four-engined development of the Calcutta flying boats, with larger wing span, enclosed cockpit and exceptionally comfortable accommodation. *British Airways*

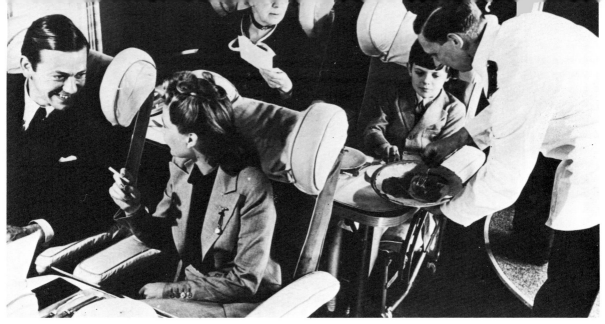

Above: The Empire flying boats afforded the kind of legroom which not even first class passengers now enjoy. Seats had individual arms and there was room for a table to be slid between the seats rather than lowered from the seat in front. Smoking was a much more acceptable habit than now. Most publicity photographs of the time had the ubiquitous pretty girl waving an unlit cigarette — even over food! *British Airways*

Below: A toast on an Empire flying boat. The days of pre-packed meals and plastic cutlery were still distant. Comfort for passengers was probably more important than now with the journeys to the Far East taking days rather than hours. When the London to Cape Town service began, in 1932, 11 days were required for the 8,539 miles. *British Airways*

Top: The early history of air transport after World War I was of a succession of optimistic ventures which generally ended in financial failure. The government was opposed to subsidies despite the fact that most other countries were subscribing at least two thirds of the operating costs of their air services. All services had ceased by February 1921 and the government reluctantly acknowledged the need to act. In 1924, four rival companies amalgamated to form Imperial Airways, which was to receive a £1m grant spread over 10 years. The de Havilland DH50 on the left was used by Imperial Airways for charter work from 1924-1932. It carried four passengers with the pilot in an open cockpit behind the cabin. On the right is a DH9C. *British Airways*

Above: When Imperial Airways was formed in 1924, the reputation of air transport for reliability and safety could hardly have been lower. It was decided that future designs must be multi-engined and so the first design from Armstrong Whitworth was a three-engined biplane called the Argosy.

Powered by direct-drive Jaguar engines, the Argosy provided seating for 20 with the captain and first officer sitting side by side in an open cockpit. G-EBOZ was not delivered new to Imperial Airways, operating for a period under Air Council ownership to test its potential as a troop carrier. The plane was handed over to Imperial Airways in April 1927 and named *City of Wellington,* later to be changed to *City of Arundel.* A shortage of aircraft for the South African route occasioned its transfer to Almaza in Egypt and G-EBOZ is seen here at Khartoum. *British Airways*

Above: The Handley Page O/700 was the shape of airliners at the beginning of the 1920s, five being built in 1919/20. After a period of operation by Handley Page Transport Ltd, one went to South Africa for use in advertising, three went to Handley Page Indo Burmese Transport Ltd, and the fifth went to China to join others as part of the Chinese government's six-strong air mail fleet. They began an experimental Peking to Tientsin service in May 1920. One aircraft was used to bomb rebels but caught fire in the air and crashed. *Handley Page*

Right: The interior of Handley Page O/700 showing internal struts, cane chairs, flowers and bracket clock. No seat belts were provided. *Handley Page*

Above: A major factor in delaying the commercial viability of civil aviation was the difficulty of night flying. Navigational aids and lighting at airports were inadequate to ensure safety. The railways had very quickly won GPO contracts from mail coach operators but it was not until 1934 that the Empire Air Mail Scheme was introduced. Throughout the 1920s, night flying was exceptional but this view of a French Farman Goliath arriving at Le Bourget after the first night flight from London was taken on 26 November 1926. *Radio Times Hulton Picture Library*

Centre left: The Armstrong Whitworth Argosy liners were replacements for the small De Haviland DH34 two-bay biplanes which seated only eight passengers. The Argosy liners carried 19 passengers and had three Armstrong Whitworth Jaguar radial engines yielding 420hp each. They could cruise at 95mph and had a maximum speed of 110mph. Argosy 1 G-EBOZ *The City of Arundel* and Argosy II G-AAEJ *The City of Coventry* are seen here at Khartoum. They were employed on the Cairo-Khartoum section of the London-Cape Town air mail route which started in February 1931. Two days were required for their 1,000-mile journey. *British Airways*

Left: The interior of an Armstrong Whitworth Argosy. Cane chairs were typical of early airliners as were the huge windows. In addition to operating between Cairo and Khartoum, these planes also flew between Croydon and Basle as the first stage of the Karachi service. *British Airways*

Above: The first Handley Page HP42 about to
leave Radlett aerodrome on a trial flight in
November 1930. Powered by four supercharged
British Jupiter engines, the plane was designed
specifically for European and eastern sections of
Empire air routes. Two versions were produced:
one for flights from Cairo to Karachi and Kisumu,
fitted with six and later 12 seats in the forward
cabin and a further 12 in the rear; and the other
for Croydon-based European flights with 18 seats
in the forward cabin and 20 in the rear. Four
aircraft of each type were produced and they
began service in June 1931. Note the newsreel
camera crew on the left and the nose-mounted
test gear including a crude 'artificial horizon'.
Radio Times Hulton Picture Library

Right: Imperial Airways' HP42 *Heracles* at
Croydon before flying to Paris with the Royal
Mail. The early years of Imperial Airways were
shaky and, for the time, heavily subsidised by the
government. No fortunes were made between the
wars by providing an air service. But the
government realised how vital were links with the
Empire and Imperial Airways concentrated on
such routes. Yet this policy did not really help the
company. In 1936, 55% of total passenger mileage
was on Empire routes but they accounted for only
10% of passengers carried. Nonetheless finances
had improved and Royal Mail contracts proved a
great impetus. In September 1939, the Croydon-
based HP42s were evacuated to Whitchurch.
They were then used to fly supplies to France from
Whitchurch and Exeter. *Heracles* was wrecked in
a gale at Whitchurch in March 1940.
British Airways

Above: The tremendous wing span of the HP42 can be clearly seen in this view of the first, *Hannibal*, at Cairo. In 1940, it was decided to recall the four eastern planes. *Hannibal* was on the return flight from Delhi in March 1940 when it disappeared between Jask in Iran and Sharjah in Trucial Oman. An intensive search was carried out but no trace of the plane was ever found. *Harry Woodman*

Below: The HP42s set new standards for quietness, furnishing and cuisine. The maximum speed was 130mph and the cruising speed 100mph. The interior still looks like a railway carriage. *Radio Times Hulton Picture Library*

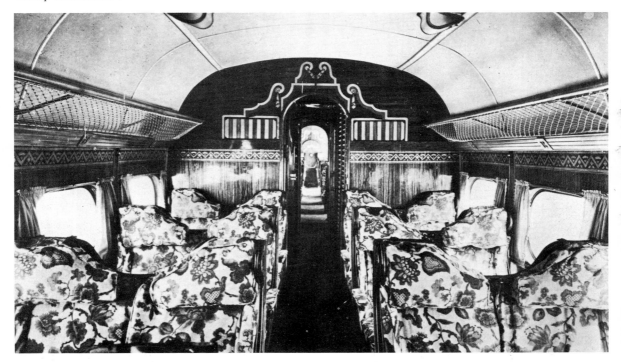

Above: Handley Page W10 G-EBMM *City of Melbourne*, one of the ugliest planes ever built. G-EBMM was based at Croydon until sold to Alan Cobham for use in air displays. To help with the first refuelling on Cobham's attempted non-stop flight to Australia in April 1934, G-EBMM was converted to a tanker.

The tanks were removed at Ford and the plane took off for Whitley. It never arrived, crashing at Aston Clinton in Buckinghamshire and was written off. Cobham took off from the Medway at Rochester accompanied by his engineer, A. B. Elliott. The destination was Melbourne and the intention to assess the commercial viability of flights to Australia. Between Baghdad and Basra, Elliott was mortally injured by shots from tribesmen. Cobham pressed on, reaching Melbourne 45 days after leaving England. On his return, Cobham landed on the Thames at Westminster and was subsequently knighted. *British Airways*

Below: Celebrating Christmas on an unknown flight aboard a Handley Page W10. Four of these planes were delivered to Imperial Airways, first appearing in 1925. They were allotted the names of cities and they entered service in March 1926, supplementing the W8s on all regular routes. Sixteen passengers could be carried at a cruising speed of 100mph. Of the four planes, three crashed leaving a sole survivor to reach a natural end — on a scrap heap in Malta. *British Airways*

DANGER THE LOAD ON THIS RUNWAY NOT TO EXCEED 1½ TONS

Above left: Croydon airport was established in 1915 and turned into a civil customs airfield in 1926. It is seen here soon after adopting its new role with Imperial Airways Handley Page biplanes in evidence. After World War II, Heathrow gained in ascendancy, bringing about the closure of Croydon in 1959. *British Airways*

Left: Re-fuelling the Tiger Moth biplane which won the King's Cup air race of 1926. The cup was presented by King George V to encourage sporting flying and it became the most important and well-known British race. A new system was

inaugurated in 1926 when the same course of four different laps was flown from Hendon on each of the two days.

The entire event covered 1,464 miles and the winner was Captain H. S. Broad in a De Havilland 60 Tiger Moth, averaging 90.4mph. *Esso*

Above: Inside a hangar at Croydon. The large biplane is Short 17 G-ACJJ *Scylla*, built at Rochester in 1933-4 for the European services of British Airways. Accommodation for 39 passengers was provided. *British Airways*

Left: This could easily be the interior of a rather spartan American-style railway sleeping coach with longitudinal bunks, but it is the interior of a German airliner c1930.
Radio Times Hulton Picture Library

Right: The galley on an Imperial Airways Short L17 which was a landplane development of the Kent flying boat.   *British Airways*

Below: In flight entertainment is not as new an idea as one might imagine. These passengers are about to see the first film ever to be shown on an aeroplane and the date was 6 April 1925 although the flight and airline were not recorded.
Radio Times Hulton Picture Library

Left: The Spirit of St. Louis was a home-made plane and Lindbergh had never flown over water before. He had to keep the cabin window open to keep himself awake and afterwards spoke of a sense of 'sleeping with my eyes open'. But his reward was 25,000 dollars put up by a New York hotel owner and a tumultuous ticker tape welcome on his return to New York. Lindbergh is seen here arriving at Croydon on 29 May 1927.
Radio Times Hulton Picture Library

Bottom left: When they have something to celebrate, the Americans have no half measures. This was the reception given to Lindbergh when he made his way up Broadway from the Battery to the City Hall, New York after his solo flight across the Atlantic.
Radio Times Hulton Picture Library

Below: Refuelling a German Junkers 130 passenger aircraft at Croydon airport in 1925. The plane had arrived with a load of bullion, delivered as part of payments made in reparation to the British government after World War I. The plane is being serviced and refuelled by the usual Pratts hand pump. Corrugated fuselages were a Junkers' hallmark. *Esso*

Top left: In September 1934, the longest flight in the world was the KLM service from Amsterdam to Batavia (Djakarta) — a distance of 9,000 miles. It was operated by what was then the fastest four-engined airliner, the unique Fokker FXXXVI, built in Amsterdam and capable of 165mph. With a crew of five, the plane carried 32 passengers on European flights and 16 on the Batavia flight, each passenger having a folding sleeping berth. The plane was sold to Scottish Aviation in 1939 and was burnt out in a take-off accident at Prestwick airport, Ayrshire, in May 1940.
Radio Times Hulton Picture Library

Above: The Railway (Air Transport) Acts of 1929 gave railway companies the freedom to invest in airlines. In April 1931, the Great Western Railway led the way, as it had done with the introduction of railway motor services, by arranging with Imperial Airways to operate on its behalf a service between Plymouth, Torquay and Cardiff (and later Birmingham). It was not a success, but early in 1934 the four major railway companies and Imperial Airways each contributed £10,000 to form Railway Air Services. Most of the new air routes were over the territory of the GWR and LMS. The location of this photograph, taken in May 1934, is not known.
Oxford Publishing Company/British Rail

Left: Imperial Airways operated a fleet of 12 of these de Havilland DH86A aircraft on European, Khartoum-West Africa and Penang-Saigon-Hong Kong routes. They came into service from 1935 and continued into the early war years. Carrying 10 passengers, the DH86A had a cruising speed of 145mph, and a range of 760 miles.
British Airways

An Imperial Airways Ensign *Ettrick* parked in front of the Control Tower at Croydon airport. These were the largest aircraft built for Imperial Airways, with a length of 114ft and a wing span of 123ft. Introduced in 1938, they were built largely in response to the need for much greater mail capacity following the decision in 1934 to remove the surcharge on air mail within the Empire. *British Airways*

Top: The de Havilland DH91 Albatross came into service in 1939, the last year of Imperial Airways operations. In the previous year, Chamberlain's government had decided that competition between Imperial Airways and British Airways, set up in 1935 through the merger of four airlines, should be ended. The two airlines were formally merged in April 1940 with Sir John Reith, former Chairman of Imperial Airways, as the first Chairman of the new organisation. The Albatross was held by many to be the most attractive aircraft of its day. Built of wood, it gave outstanding performance with a cruising speed of 210mph which enabled it to capture the Croydon-Paris-Brussels records in 1939. *British Airways*

Above: The Duchess of Bedford (1865-1937) being helped into her flying suit by her pilot on the occasion of the Lord Northesk Cup Competition for women pilots at Reading on 8 August 1936. The Duchess, wife of the 11th Duke, believed that flying was good for her deafness, learned to pilot a plane and in 1929 flew to Karachi and back in eight days. In the following year she completed the 19,000-mile trip to Cape Town and back in 19½ days. *Radio Times Hulton Picture Library*

Above: Foreshadowing the way in which aeroplanes were to revolutionise the nature of war in 1939-45, planes stand by at Croydon airport in readiness to fly at a moment's notice to Prague following the announcement that British residents had been warned to leave. The date is 23 September 1938. On the previous day, Hitler had informed Chamberlain that he wanted immediate occupation of the Sudetenland area of Czechoslovakia, not to wait until after negotiations.
Radio Times Hulton Picture Library

Below: Neville Chamberlain making his 'peace in our time' speech at Heston airport on his return from meeting Hitler in Munich. Air travel has given international relations a more personal character, enabling politicians to meet with much greater frequency. In the background is the British Airways Super Electra which transported Chamberlain. The airline owned seven Lockheed 10A Electras and they inaugurated the express Viking mail and passenger service to Stockholm in 1937. The creation of British Airways in 1935 gave the government an opportunity to re-appraise its policy towards air transport and the new airline was accepted as the government's second 'chosen instrument'. Imperial Airways were pressed to relinquish certain European services and British Airways was soon entrusted with most subsidised services to Northern Europe and the development of services to West Africa and South America.
British Airways

Travel in the
TWENTIES
and
THIRTIES

ROAD TRAVEL

Above: Six LCC trams converge at the Elephant and Castle in 1922. There were 123 miles of conduit-equipped lines run by the LCC but later construction and suburban lines reverted to the more usual overhead-trolley system, necessitating changeover points where the conduit passed outside the rails into an open pit. Ploughs could be removed or inserted and the trolleys raised or lowered. *Radio Times Hulton Picture Library*

Left: Holborn looking east in 1920 with two London City Council cars. The LCC tramways were unique in the 1920s and 1930s in adhering to the already unusual conduit system whereby positive and negative conductors were enclosed in an underground tunnel. A plough projected from the underneath of the car through a slot centrally positioned between the rails and this carried shoes to provide electrical contact. It was a costly system to construct and maintain and was only adopted as a result of opposition to overhead wires on aesthetic grounds. It must be agreed that this scene would be much less attractive with a plethora of tram poles and wires.
National Motor Museum

Right: An unusual facility provided in the one man trams of London United Tramways was the locator which informed passengers of their whereabouts in the absence of a conductor. The date is February 1922.
Radio Times Hulton Picture Library

Below: The familiar one-man buses of our time are not a recent concept as this picture on a one-man London United Tramways car of 1922 indicates. The care and pride taken over the appearance of trams may be seen in the ornate lining and decoration on the side of the car.
Radio Times Hulton Picture Library

Above: A Feltham tram and S-type bus of 1920 near Ealing Broadway station. The steam tram, so common in northern industrial cities, was never used in London so apart from a few experimental battery cars and two cable lines, the whole of London's pre-electric network was horse-operated.
London Transport

Left: Some annoyance as well as pleasure was evidently caused to the rate-payers by the decision of West Ham to spend £1,000 celebrating the coming of age of its tramway system in February 1925 since the network had lost £58,000 in the previous year. It was a dense network with probably more route miles per square mile than almost any other system. This decorated tram boasts that 66 million miles had been run and 842 million passengers carried since the system opened.
Radio Times Hulton Picture Library

Left: In 1926 a joint service was established by Croydon Corporation and London County Council undertaking joint working between Purley and the Embankment. As the LCC cars were heavier, this entailed the relaying of the track which can be seen here in progress in London Road, Norbury.
Ian Allan Library

Below left: One of the problems of trams vis-a-vis buses was the chaos caused when a tram derailed or broke down. Buses can divert around the obstacle. Trams obviously cannot. A derailment has caused this scene of congestion on Blackfriars Road on 11 January 1930.
Radio Times Hulton Picture Library

Above right: LCC trams on the Embankment by what was then Charing Cross underground station (now Embankment) in October 1933. The Embankment line linked Westminster and Blackfriars Bridge by what was in effect a reserved track. By making an ideal terminal loop in both directions for the southern routes of the LCC, the line carried a continuous procession of trams bound for every part of South London from Abbey Wood to Kew Bridge. *London Transport*

Right: Trams in the Mile End Road looking east. The changeover point between conduit and overhead trolley contact may be seen to the left of the nearest tram. The conduit can be seen passing outside the rail. The date is April 1934.
London Transport

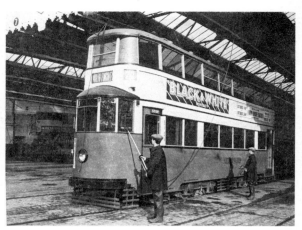

Left: Vauxhall Cross was the intersection of a number of tram routes. If the system in the photograph, taken in August 1936, looks complicated, it was made even more so by works carried on in 1938. *London Transport*

Top: Cleaning a Metropolitan Feltham car with a high pressure hose and brush in March 1939. The Feltham cars were introduced in 1930, a hundred being built for the MET and London United Tramways. Ninety of London's Feltham cars were sold to Leeds after the last routes were closed in 1952. The war gave a temporary reprieve to London's tram network but the London Transport Executive decided in 1948 that there was no place for the tram in postwar London.
London Transport

Above: The General Strike of May 1926 was an opportunity for all would-be engine, bus and tram drivers to test their abilities and many did not let it pass. After being shut for 10 days, the first LCC tram out of New Cross ran on 14 May with a volunteer at the controls. Feelings were evidently running high with the union jack and hats being waved. *Radio Times Hulton Picture Library*

Right: Two volunteer drivers work a tram in Hammersmith Broadway on 14 May 1926. Many of the volunteers were university students. There is no doubt that the lorry considerably reduced the impact of the General Strike. Had the country had to rely on the easily disrupted railways for the transport of food, the outcome might have been very different.
Radio Times Hulton Picture Library

Below: A Plymouth Corporation tram protected by boards and wire netting during the General Strike. There were $17\frac{1}{2}$ miles of tramway in Plymouth, operated by a maximum of 184 cars. Routes were gradually replaced by buses between 1930-39 except for one which lasted until 1945.
Radio Times Hulton Picture Library

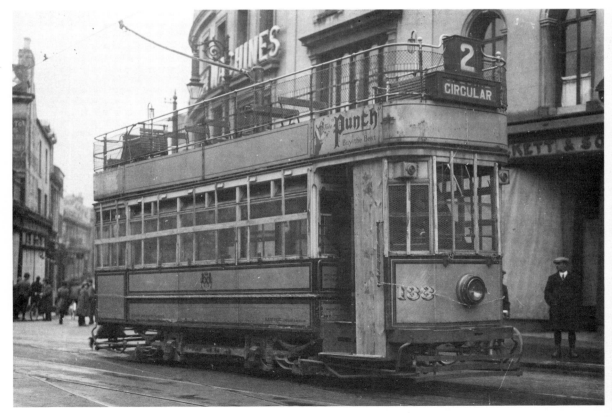

Above: Most tram systems were urban, or later suburban, concerns but a few ran largely through countryside and served relatively small communities. The Burton & Ashby Light Railway, owned by the Midland and later LMS railways, was a good example. Another, but built largely for tourist traffic, was the Douglas Head Marine Drive tramway on the Isle of Man. Built to standard gauge and opened in 1896, it ran for three miles from the tourist focal point at Douglas Head to Port Soderick. The line closed as usual at the end of the 1939 season but never reopened and much of the track bed is now covered by rock falls. Some idea of the spectacular nature of the journey is given by this view of car No 5 crossing Walberry Viaduct on 30 May 1939.
W. A. Camwell

Left: Trams were essentially urban conveyances but occasionally a route was extended to serve the suburbs. Generally the bus performed this duty. This attractive scene of a tram in Reddish, Lancashire reminds one that even the suburbs enjoyed tranquility before the motor car destroyed it. The rattling passage of the tram on its rails embedded in cobbles was a brief affair, accompanied by a cheerful bell rather than the blare of hooters.
Radio Times Hulton Picture Library

FLAT
To LET
APPLY
TURNBULL PARNIE
& ADAM
211 HOPE ST.

ANNAN 30-240

Below: Trams in Argyle Street, Glasgow, which was one of the last cities to dispense with trams. Britain has perhaps been more ruthless than most European countries in tearing up tram lines. Most foreign capital cities still retain what is the cleanest and most environmentally acceptable form of mass urban transport. In Britain, the tide turned for the tram in 1928 when the first tram service was replaced by a bus — in Manchester — although tram lines had already begun to be abandoned and between 1924-33, about a third of the country's route tram mileage was closed.
G. A. Oliver

Top: Trams in Princes Street, Edinburgh c1924. The tram system in Edinburgh began operation in the 1870s and part of it was operated on the cable system whereby the trams were drawn by cables running in conduits beneath the road and driven by stationary engines at stragetic points. The longest cable was $6\frac{1}{2}$ miles which required innumerable horizontal pulleys to guide it round corners and vertical ones to support the cable in its conduit. It was the fourth largest cable system in the world, being exceeded only by those of San Francisco, Kansas City and Melbourne. Conversion to overhead electrification took place in the 1920s. The system remained intact until 1952 when a major change in policy began replacement by buses. The last tram ran in 1957.
G. Oliver

Above: Trams crossing Jamaica Bridge, Glasgow c1934. The Glasgow system was the largest in Scotland and built to 4ft $7\frac{3}{4}$in gauge to allow railway wagons to use the tram lines. Because the depth of a flange of a railway wheel is greater than the depth of a groove in a tram rail, the wagons had to run on their flanges rather than their tyres. The Corporation was one of the pioneers of electric traction, converting or withdrawing the whole fleet of 385 horse trams by 1902. Until 1945, the various tram routes were colour coded, the upper decks of the cars being painted in different colours. As late as 1955, short extensions to Glasgow's system were being built.
G. A. Oliver

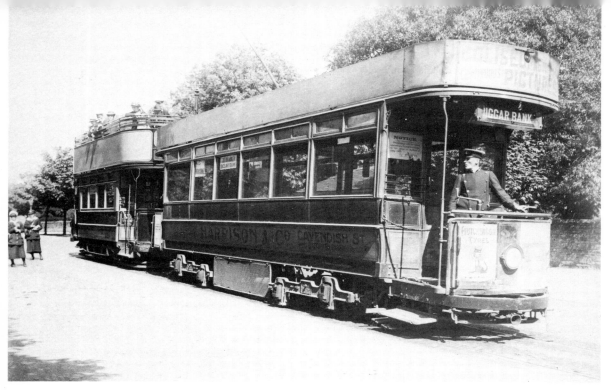

Above: A tandem tram in Abbey Lane, Barrow-in-Furness. The Barrow tram system was a small 4ft gauge operation worked by the British Electric Traction Co Ltd, until 1920 when it was taken over by the Corporation. The ability to attach a trailer car to the power car was one of the advantages of trams over buses. *R. Sankey*

Right: The flexibility of buses and their low capital cost ensured their gradual victory over the tram. The price of fuel and the need for cleaner modes of transport did not become influencing factors in transport policy until after most tram systems were closed and dismantled. The small network at Barrow was a early casualty, being closed on 5 April 1932. The last tram is seen here before its final run. *R. Sankey*

Above: Traffic in Euston Road passing Somers Town Goods station, adjacent to Gilbert Scott's hotel at St Pancras station, and now the site of the new British Library. Two S-type buses are passing. The growth of bus traffic in the capital was prodigious. From 1,000 buses in 1908, the figure grew to 3,522 by 1913. The adoption of the pneumatic tyre was the most important improvement of the 1920s, reducing costs from 4d a mile for the solid tyre in 1906 to 0.10d per mile in 1932. *National Motor Museum*

Below: A K-type of 1919 is flanked by an NS-type on the left and an early ST-type on the right. NS1 was built with a covered top deck but the Metropolitan Police scotched the idea and the first examples took to the streets of London with the usual open top. A more lenient attitude prevailed at the end of 1925 and the days of the familiar open top General bus were numbered as the first covered tops arrived. However, the staircase was still exposed to the elements. The ST came into its own during World War II when it was discovered that its engine was well suited for conversion to coal gas operation to help to reduce London Transport petrol consumption. Exercising a horse on the road around Marble Arch even then does not look unduly safe. *London Transport*

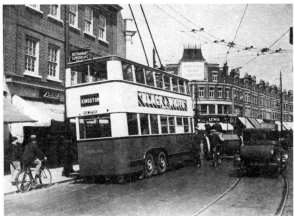

Above: Trolleybuses were an attempt to retain electricity as a motive power, using former tram wires and poles in many cases. It has sadly proved to be only a delay to the eventual dominance of the diesel engine, although trolley buses were still operating in Bradford until the early 1970s. A London United trolley bus is seen here on the Kingston-on-Thames route in May 1931. *Ian Allan Library*

Left: Trams and buses at Elephant and Castle in July 1934. A later ST is on the left and in the centre an LT type No 1334. A third axle naturally facilitated a greater carrying capacity. The first of the type had exposed staircases but by the time LT 1334 was built, they were enclosed necessitating some reduction in seating capacity. In the previous year, the London Passenger Transport Board had been formed embracing all bus, tram and tube undertakings and ending competition. Until 1923, when the London Traffic Act attempted to regulate routes, schedules and safety regulations on bus operators, it had been very much a free-for-all. *London Transport*

Below : The Mid Suffolk Motor Bus Service vehicle on the right has a chassis built by AEC, formed in 1912, and served between Dereham, Stonham, Ipswich, Stowmarket and Bury St. Edmunds. The unidentified F. G. Elliott bus served Stonham and district and the photograph was taken in Earl Stonham. Competition, particularly amongst urban and suburban operators, was fierce, leap-frogging a rival between bus stops to poach customers being common. Many one bus (and one lorry) concerns were set up after World War I by demobbed soldiers with war savings.
Suffolk Photographic Survey

Bottom : A Crossley bus outside a 'practical boot repairer', probably in Ipswich since the charabancs's owners, JDW Transport, did and still do operate from that town. Despite the windscreen, summer flies obviously make the driver feel a need for goggles.
Suffolk Photographic Society

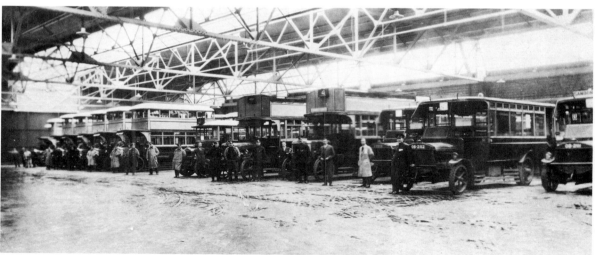

Top: Schoolchildren boarding Crosville buses. The rural bus doubtless made the journey to the village school very much easier for children in isolated communities but in turn it has made possible the creation of monolithic establishments in towns, served by school buses. The intimate village school is now almost a thing of the past.
Crosville Motor Services

Above: The interior of Harborne Garage, Birmingham, in 1926 showing AEC 503 double-deckers,Tilling Stevens double-deckers and Daimler CK single-deckers.
West Midlands Passenger Transport Authority

Above: Four AEC 503 double-deckers receiving carefully-posed attention at Harborne Garage in 1928. Birmingham's trams survived until the early 1950s but the municipal bus services developed rapidly to serve the growing car factories, before the days when practically every worker owned a car.
West Midlands Passenger Transport Authority

Right: The lower saloon of a 54-seat double-decker of which one hundred were built in 1935 by Metropolitan Cammell and Birmingham Railway Carriage and Wagon on a Daimler chassis.
West Midlands Passenger Transport Authority

Below: Crosville charabancs at one of the Elan Valley dams near Rhayder, built by Birmingham Water Dept to supply the burgeoning city. Like the motor car, the charabanc and bus opened up new venues for the sightseer, heralding the end of rural peace and solitude for villages and areas blessed with exceptional charm.
Crosville Motor Services

Bottom: Two charabancs convey TUC delegates to Dartmoor during the 1923 conference in Plymouth. In much the same way as mail coaches influenced early railway carriage design, the first open buses owed design details to railway practice, such as the door shape and handles and the solebar construction. The maximum speed was 12mph. *TUC Library*

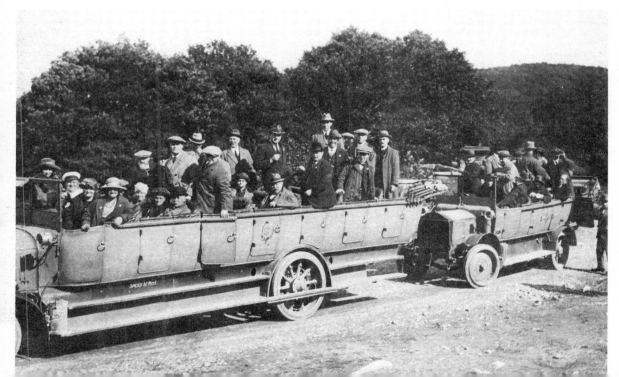

Top: In 1935, the Cyclists' Touring Club celebrated its Jubilee and to mark the occasion a relay of cyclists travelled through England, Wales and Scotland bearing a message for the King which was signed by the Lord Mayors and Lord Provosts of the principal towns. Engrossed on vellum the message reminded King George V that he had been a patron of the CTC for 25 years. Lord Cottenham is seen here sending off the first relay of cyclists from the Mansion House in March 1935. *Radio Times Hulton Picture Library*

Above: Between the wars, cycling as recreation perhaps reached its apogee. Cycling clubs proliferated and in 1931 the National Cyclists' Union organised its first annual rally and gymkhana at the Alexandra Palace. A group of cyclists is seen arriving for the rally in June 1934. *Radio Times Hulton Picture Library*

Top: In 1937, the quad bicycle was introduced, costing £50 and claimed to be capable of 60mph. This example was photographed in Wandsworth.
Radio Times Hulton Picture Library

Above: In May 1938, the Southern Railway instigated the idea of a cyclists' excursion by running a special train with five vans for cycles to Winchester for the New Forest.
Radio Times Hulton Picture Library

82

Above left: Ferodo employees on motorcycles outside their factory in Chapel-en-le-Frith. The probable owners are sitting on the wall in the background. Driving motorcycles of some power is one area which has remained an almost exclusively male preserve and doubtless these girls thought the pose quite risqué for the time. The two machines on the left are Coventry-built Rudges and that on the right is unidentified.

In 1928 a Standard Rudge capable of 60mph from 15bhp cost £46. *Ferodo Limited*

Left: How it all began: this view of a 1896/9 Benz and a tricycle seems to capture the nature of the internal combustion engine revolution. The face of the young man in the Benz suggests an unquestioning optimism about the future role of the car while the old man on the tricycle seems aware that the new fangled machine poses a threat to his way of life. It is a strange paradox that the Victorians achieved a greater technical advancement than any corresponding period

before them and yet they were capable of scornful scepticism over so many inventions. The motor car did not escape the mockery of pundits, pictures being taken of a car beside a huge steam engine as though to ridicule the claims made by its protagonists. *National Motor Museum*

Above: The bus and motor car were directly responsible for the spread of ribbon development. It was no longer necessary to live on a railway or tram route and a view of fields at the back was preferable to a place in town. The harm done to the environment was recognised by the Restriction of Ribbon Development Act of 1935 but by 1939, it was acknowledged that that Act had failed to achieve its aim. It was not long before builders developed the green fields behind the first ribbon of houses and suburbia became a new phenomenon. A Morris Cowley saloon in a typical surburban street with privet hedge and black and white path tiles in 1927.
National Motor Museum

Above: An early publicity photograph of a six-cylinder Morris Isis. The ability to leave the bustle of the town and find tranquility in the English countryside has always been a major theme in car advertising. So too has been the idea that the fair sex appreciate the man who can drive them about, preferably in some style. It was probably this approach to the car and its attributes which led to it becoming the status symbol of the Twentieth Century, par excellence. As early as 1920, the future Lord Asquith, who was then the government's chief industrial advisor, warned that the manifestation of wealth in the form of ostentatious expenditure on motor cars was one of the reasons for the current industrial unrest. The people's car had yet to appear. *British Leyland*

Above right: Until the advent of roll-on, roll-off car ferries, taking one's car across the water was a more adventurous business. The GWR steamer service from Fishguard to Rosslare catered for the passenger who wished to tour Ireland in his own car — the days of readily available car hire were still distant. The car being loaded is a BSA. The other three cars, from left to right are a Ford Eight, still selling for as little as £100 in 1935-37, a Lanchester, absorbed by Daimler during the depression, and a Riley.
British Rail/Oxford Publishing Company

Right: Beneath the walls of Conway Castle, built largely between 1283 and 1287, a pair of Model T Fords and three unidentified cars illustrate the way tourism was transformed by the motor car. Only by reading travel diaries written before their creation can one appreciate the paradox that although holidays were more limited in scope without them, visitors explored the area much more throughly, dependent though they were on foot, horse-drawn bus or train. Today's walkers and cyclists will readily understand.
National Motor Museum

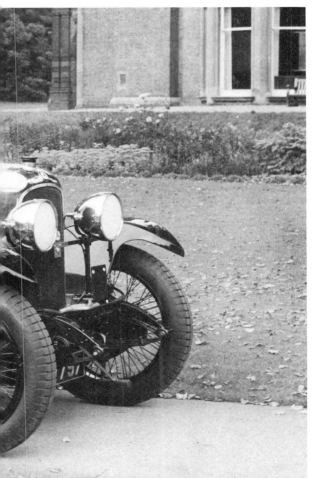

Top left: Traffic in Braemar for the 1934 Gathering, held every August and one of the most celebrated Highland games. The desire of motorists and passengers to enjoy open air or well ventilated motoring was almost universal, judging by the ability to slide or remove at least part if not all the roof on most vehicles, cars and charabancs alike. The trend towards fixed tops cannot be blamed entirely on Ralph Nader and his influence: denser traffic has made clean air harder to find and one has to be a diehard to find any joy amongst juggernaut fumes on main roads.
D. C. Thomson & Co

Left: The Vauxhall 30/98 was in production from 1919 — 26 and marked the virtual beginning of the postwar sporting breed in Britain. It had a $4\frac{1}{2}$ litre four-cylinder side valve engine and wide ratio four-speed gearbox. The 30/98 gave a good account of itself in hill climbs and shorter races at Brooklands, but it was overtaken by its younger rival, the Bentley, and Vauxhall's sporting image went into decline after General Motors bought the company in 1925. The 30/98 seen here has a tourer body. *Vauxhall Motors Ltd*

Above: Taxis for hire in Ixworth, Suffolk. On the left are two Model T Fords. In 1922, only one person in every 78 owned a motor car and rural bus services were still in their infancy, so the taxi was a vital part of rural transport, carrying people to and from the railway station. Not many years earlier, these taxis would have been horses and traps. *Suffolk Photographic Survey*

Top: One of the leading car photographers of the 1930s was a man named Brunel. This delightful scene in the Exmoor village of Exford is typical of his work and the horseman may well have stood there on request. The car is his Talbot 14/45. The absence of yellow lines, parking notices and the usual plethora of traffic signs which have often been allowed to disfigure our villages is noteworthy. *National Motor Museum*

Above: In the days when it was exceptional for people to leave their home town, the works' outing had a much greater significance than it does today. Even in 1939 less than half the population left home even for a single night during the year. Here the Lancia motor fleet of Messrs Robinson of Scarborough is about to take the managers and their wives of W. H. Smith & Son, LNER No 5 District, on a tour Thorntondale and the Forge Valley. W. H. Smith was then largely a station bookstall concern — hence the division into railway districts. The party lunched at the Grand Hotel to the playing of the resident orchestra, followed by speeches and toasts to 'The King' and 'The Firm'. *W. H. Smith & Son*

Above: An early pump installation at the City Garage, Winchester. In the winter of 1919/20, the Anglo-American Oil Company (as Esso Petroleum was then known) pioneered the kerbside pump delivery system in England. These first pumps were worked with a long crank handle and delivered one, two or five gallons according to size; delivery into the motorist's tank being registered by a dial indicator. The underground tanks were of various capacities, from 500 to 1,000 gallons. The car being filled up here is a Sunbeam. Note the charabanc which appears to be owned by the garage. *Esso*

Below: This view of an unidentified filling station in 1936 recalls the days when it was customary to sell several brands of petrol, in this case Essolene, National Benzole, Shell, Esso Ethyl and Power. Oil companies have been unusually consistent in their corporate logo design, Esso, Castrol and Shell still using the same style. *National Motor Museum*

Above: William Morris was the archetypal self-made man although of an essentially post-Victorian nature. The son of a farm bailiff, he was obliged to support his family from an early age and he graduated through bicycles and motorbikes to selling, repairing and hiring motor cars. Progress from his first designs in 1910 to the appearance at the 1912 Motor Show of the Morris Oxford was rapid. By introducing volume production to the car industry, his cars were very competitively-priced and orders for the Oxford necessitated the immediate leasing of the old Military Academy at Cowley with a view to producing 1,500 cars a year. Morris created the production line and in 1920, when this view of the finishing shop was taken, 1,550 cars were produced. By 1935, it was 104,000, a third of the British output. On the left are Morris Cowleys and on the right Morris Oxfords.
National Motor Museum

Left: The production line at Cowley in the days when cars still had chassis and before such production systems destroyed the vital element of pride in the finished product. However, as early as 1923, unmanned machines were introduced at the Morris engine works in Cowley. Designed to machine cylinder blocks, they were the first example of automation but they were not a success and manually operated processes were reinstated. It has taken just over 50 years from that first experiment to the entire production of a car being entrusted to unmanned machines.
British Leyland

Above: The railways obviously enabled many city workers to visit the country or seaside on one of the innumerable excursions which the railway companies organised throughout the summer. But the motor car gave unprecedented freedom and mobility and opened up beauty spots remote from a railway. Visiting country houses became a more common pleasure, although the day when taxation and soaring maintenance costs would compel some owners to turn their grounds into menageries was still distant. In 1926 the Council for the Preservation of Rural England was set up in response to the growing need to protect the countryside from the kind of harm caused by sheer weight of numbers and sometimes the thoughtlessness of people unaccustomed to country ways. A seafront rally in the 1930s. On the left is a Talbot 14/45, on the right a Rolls and behind an Austin 7. The Hon Charles Rolls was one of the few progressive men of wealth who realised the potential of the car and backed their beliefs with capital. In 1904 he met Henry Royce, an electrical engineer, in Manchester to see Royce's twin-cylinder 1.8 litre prototype. The outcome was the forging of the two names in the following year to produce a marque which has become a byword for quality. Just a year later, in 1906, Rolls won the Isle of Man TT race for catalogue touring cars in a four-litre 'Light Twenty'. The Silver Ghost appeared in 1907 and were snapped up by the kind of clientele who have patronised the make ever since — monarchs, millionaires, sheiks and maharajahs.
National Motor Museum

Below: Bugatti set up his own factory at Molsheim just before World War I and went on to produce some of the most successful and eccentric sports cars of the interwar years. The classic Type 51 was the first Bugatti to have twin overhead camshafts, long adopted by Alfa Romeo, Bugatti's main rival in the 1930s. For the French Grand Prix at Tours in 1923, Bugatti produced perhaps the most unlikely looking racing car with a tank body and two litre engine. It made third place. Bugatti built up a loyal following; the marque's Owners' Club has been one of the most active. A meeting of the Club is seen here at the Cotswold village of Broadway. *National Motor Museum*

Above: Miss J. MacDonald and F. O. Roberts in an Austin Seven Swallow, during the 1930 TUC Congress which was held at Nottingham. The Swallow Side Car Co began business in Blackpool and took up building elegant sports bodywork for modest chassis such as the Standard, Swift, Fiat, Morris Cowley and Austin Seven. Swallow advertising blurb revealed that 'these bodies transform the Austin into a real car'! The company later moved down to Coventry where its leading light, Bill Lyons, founded Jaguar.
TUC Library

Right: A corollary of automobile construction based on chassis was the business of coachbuilding which gave tremendous scope for fine craftsmanship. In the fifties, bodies tended to be designed for only the more expensive cars. Before World War II that was far from true, companies producing special bodies for cars throughout the price range. This is an example of what could be done for the well-heeled client, in this case the Maharajah of Bharatpur who commissioned Graham White to produce special coachwork for a 1920 Daimler 45hp chassis. When complete, it was described by *The Motor* magazine as 'the most luxurious and completely equipped car in the world'. The exterior of the car was painted mauve with a gold stripe while the interior was finished in solid mahogany and satin veneer, inlaid with mother of pearl. Amongst the car's equipment were a solid silver cigar box, electric fan and glass ventilators in the roof which opened outwards. On the doors of the two cabinets on either side of the settee were Dictograph mouthpieces moulded in solid silver. The cabinet on the left contained various cut-glass and silver mounted toilet bottles, a manicure set, and brush and comb and that on the right contained two large thermos flasks.
National Motor Museum

Above: Opened in 1907, Brooklands was the first circuit built specially for motor car competition in the world. The Junior Car Club organised a 200-mile race at the circuit for light cars under 1,500cc and the grid is seen here just before the 1921 race. Until 1924 no silencers were fitted but local residents forced their introduction in that year. Opposition from the wealthy Weybridge commuter belt bedevilled Brooklands' existence and was instrumental in its closure.
National Motor Museum

Centre left: At one point the famous banking at Brooklands passed near to the London & South Western Railway. This view was taken during the Brooklands Double Twelve race in 1929.
National Motor Museum

Left: An early view of the banking at Brooklands, probably taken in the early 1920s.
National Motor Museum

Left: The first French Grand Prix was held at Le Mans in 1906, won by a Renault with no less than 12,970cc. As late as 1921, Le Mans was largely unsurfaced by anything but large stones and punctures were the driver's main concern. By 1927, when this unknown race was held, it was beginning to take on the appearance of a permanent circuit. The three cars nearest the camera are Bentleys and number 4 is an Aries. *Autocar*

Top: Three Talbot Darracqs outside the KLG spark plug factory office in Robin Hood Gate, Kingston, Surrey, just before the 1921 200-mile race at Brooklands. The firm was named after Kenelm Lee Guiness who is seen on the extreme left. Second from the right is Sir Henry Seagrave who died in 1930 on Lake Windermere trying to better his own world speed record on water. *Smiths Industries*

Above: Kenelm Lee Guiness at the wheel of the Sunbeams that helped to make Brooklands famous. The circuit was built in 1906 near Weybridge as a testing ground for cars. During World War I, an aeroplane factory was built in the centre of the circuit which finally closed in 1946. *Smiths Industries*

Left: By the time Parry Thomas took the world land speed record of 171mph on Pendine sands in Wales in 1926, the possibility of breaking records with a modified production car or engine had gone. Thereafter only special cars stood any hope. *Babs*, as Thomas' Higham was called, is seen here at Brooklands in 1926. Powered by a Liberty V12 aero engine, *Babs* was built up on an ex-Zborowski chassis. Malcolm Campbell took the record from Thomas and in an attempt to reach 180mph Thomas was killed when *Babs* turned over. *Smiths Industries*

Centre left: Bonneville Salt Flats was the favourite speed competition ground before World War II, seen here with the car made at Brooklands by Reid Railton for John Cobb. Two 1,250bhp Napier Lion engines powered the four wheels and the car weighed only 65cwt. Before the war, Cobb reached 369mph and after it 400mph. It was almost the end of wheel-driven records, Donald Campbell achieving 403mph in a new Bluebird before the future passed to jet propulsion and computer-calculated aerodynamics. *Mobil Library*

Above: Malcolm Campbell held the record between 1931 and 1935, lifting it to over 300mph in his Rolls-Royce-powered *Bluebird* at Bonneville Salt Flats in the USA. *Esso*

Left: Sir Malcolm Campbell was a pilot with the Royal Flying Corps during World War I and devoted his energies thereafter to breaking speed records on land and water. In 1937 he captured the world water speed record from the USA, reaching 129.5mph. In 1938 when this view of *Bluebird* was taken, he edged it up to 130.93mph. In the following year, with a new Rolls-Royce powered *Bluebird*, he achieved 141.75mph on Lake Coniston. He died in 1948, still holding the record. By 1959 his son Donald Campbell had reached 260.35mph. *Radio Times Hulton Picture Library*

Above: In 1921, four disabled American ex-servicemen set out on a journey which took them over 130,000 miles in this car through 'practically every civilised country in the world'. As evidence of their travels, they collected automobile licence plates, coins, stamps and other bric-a-brac. When this picture was taken in May 1925, the four men were on their way to Maine and Boston where the car was destined to be placed in the Smithsonian Institute for two years and then in the Free Museum at Washington as a memorial to the disabled war veterans.
Radio Times Hulton Picture Library

Above right: Thankfully there were (and still are) places on earth where the internal combustion engine is of little help and horse or Shank's mare prevail. Such a region in 1924 was the Colombian ice field of Canada, lying midway between Alberta and British Columbia in the Canadian Rockies. This expedition was led by a Mr Harmen who had devoted 21 years to photographing the Rockies. The expedition is seen climbing the Whiterabbit pass. *Radio Times Hulton Picture Library*

Right: The European aristocracy by virtue of its wealth and leisure was inevitably responsible for much exploration down the centuries, often with an ulterior motive. The colonisation and organisation of what we now call the Third World largely ended the scope for such opportunism and the Victorian era saw the emergence of a new spirit of exploration founded on such questionable notions as the noble savage. The aristocracy were still instigating expeditions in 1926 when Count Byron Kuhn de Prorok arranged a Franco-American trip across the Sahara. The automobile caravan composed of Renault 'special purpose' vehicles is seen emerging from the Atlas mountains. *Radio Times Hulton Picture Library*

Above: An expedition organised and funded by the State of Denver leaves the City Hall, Cape Town for the Kalahari to study the history of bush tribesmen. Wealthy amateurs like Sir Richard Burton had been mixing with natives long before this expedition, but the study of anthropology was becoming a respectacle science, helped by the development of cinematography. One of this team was a 'motion picture expert'.
Radio Times Hulton Picture Library

Right: By the time World War II began, there were not many hazardous or difficult 'first' journeys which had not been successfully completed. The internal combustion engine had opened up new horizons for explorers and a generation which valued the pioneering spirit. Expeditions were mounted as readily as joint-stock companies had been floated before the South Sea Bubble. But in many countries where European colonial rule was still the order of the day, the car conveyed prestige and probably not much else given the state of the roads as seen in this view of a car about to take a rise in Basutoland in November 1923. Now renamed Lesotho, the roads still look like this, but Land Rovers are better able to cope with them than this frail machine.
Radio Times Hulton Picture Library

Travel in the
TWENTIES
and
THIRTIES

SEA
TRAVEL

Below: The *Mauretania* (31,000 tons) was a product of the Edwardian era, making her maiden voyage in 1907, but she plied the Atlantic for almost 30 years. She and her sister ship, the *Lusitania*, steamed at only a couple of knots slower than *Queen Elizabeth II* and the crossing took the same five days. The ships set a new pattern of elegance, symbolised by being the first Atlantic liners on which dressing for dinner in the first class was obligatory. Named after ancient Roman Morocco and Algeria, the *Mauretania* was naturally coal-fired when built, but converted to oil-burning after World War I, ending the most arduous work ever associated with the production of steam, feeding marine coal-fired boilers. She is seen here arriving at Liverpool Docks in December 1926 for overhaul.
Radio Times Hulton Picture Library

Right: The 24,000 ton P&O liner *Stratheden* is launched at the Barrow-in-Furness shipyard of Vickers-Armstrong by the Duchess of Buccleuch on 10 June 1937. The *Stratheden* was the fourth of the five 'Strath' liners of the 1930s, being ordered as an improvement of the *Strathmore*. With her sisters, she operated the fortnightly UK/Australia mail service although she was cruising in home waters when war broke out. Her service as a troopship was uneventful and she returned to Barrow for reconditioning in 1949

before resuming the Australian service. In 1963, the last Australian voyage was made and in the following year she was sold to John S. Latsis of Piraeus for use as a pilgrim ship in eastern waters. She was sold in 1969 and broken up at La Spezia, the chief naval harbour of Italy. *P&O*

Below right: The *Strathallan* was launched from the Vickers-Armstrong yard at Barrow-in-Furness in 1937 and is seen here at Barrow after being handed over to P&O in March 1938. In common with her sisters, she operated the fortnightly UK/Australia service but was also used as a cruise ship. When war broke out she was cruising from Australia and New Zealand to Fiji and was requisitioned as a troopship. With the older *Viceroy of India*, she helped with Operation Torch — the first Algerian landings in the North African campaign. On her second trip to Algeria, from the Clyde, she was torpedoed just after passing through the Straits of Gibraltar. Four men died in the engine room which was struck by the torpedo but the ship was taken in tow by an escorting destroyer and almost reached Oran. She sank within twelve miles of her destination but the 4,250 troops and nurses and the crew were safely taken off. The *Strathallan* was the fourth P&O liner lost in six weeks in the North African campaign. *R. Sankey*

Right: The history of P&O began in 1836 when two London merchants chartered a vessel to trade with Spain. With the acquisition of mail contracts to Lisbon, Cadiz and Gibraltar and later to Alexandria, the company prospered and grew as the main shipping company to the east. Its original title of Peninsula Steam Navigation Company was extended to include the evocative word 'Oriental' to reflect its new role. Until the opening of the Suez Canal in 1870, the mails were taken overland from Alexandria to Suez and thence to India. Hong Kong, Singapore and Sydney soon became destinations and by the 1920s, the company was one of the largest shipping lines in the world. This view shows the tourist class lounge aboard the *Stratheden*, which carried 450 tourist and 530 first class passengers. *P&O*

Below: Deck games aboard the P&O liner *Viceroy of India* (19,684 tons) which entered service in 1929 and was the first large British vessel with turbo-electric motors and compressors. Their success encouraged adoption of similar installations in the first 'Strath' class ships. Originally intended to be named *Taj Mahal*, the *Viceroy of India* was a 'one-off' design for the Bombay service on which she broke the record to London, taking 16 days, 1 hour and 42 minutes. Unusually, all cabins were single berth with interconnecting doors, and 415 first and 258 second class passengers were looked after by a crew of 417. In 1940, the ship was requisitioned as a troopship and took part in Operation Torch on the North African Coast, landing troops and vehicles at Algiers. She left on the evening of 10 November 1942 and was torpedoed the following morning, all but four of the 454 passengers and crew being saved by the destroyer HMS *Boadicea*. *P&O*

Below: The tourist class swimming pool aboard the *Stratheden* in the late 1930s. Most of the facilities associated with the modern cruise ship were in use by World War II — often in a more luxurious form than today.   *P&O*

Bottom: A P&O cruise poster of the 1930s, by which time cruising had become a popular way of taking a leisurely holiday abroad. The middle classes were becoming almost as adventurous as the aristocracy had been in the 19th century and the marketing strategy was changed to enable people with lower budgets to visit foreign parts. The 'invention' of cruising is attributed to one Arthur Anderson who, in 1835, extolled the delights of cruising round Iceland and the Faroes in the 'Shetland Journal' which he founded. Thackeray toured the Levant and Holy Land at P&O's expense in the 1840s but he used several vessels. In 1881, the first cruise around the world was made by the former P&O ship SS *Ceylon* but it was not until 1889 that regular cruises round the Mediterranean, Norwegian Fjords, and the West Indies were offered by the Orient Line.   *P&O*

Above: On 26 September 1934, RMS *Queen Mary* was launched at John Brown's yard on Clydeside. She was intended to be the first of two ships which, by virtue of their speed and size, would enable Cunard White Star to operate a weekly service to New York with two rather than the usual three vessels, the *Aquitania*, *Berengaria* and *Mauretania*. Built at a time of depression, the *Queen Mary* was made possible by a £3 million loan from the government to Cunard. She was naturally launched by Queen Mary, accompanied by King George V.   *R. Sankey*

Below: Queen Mary leaves Southampton on her maiden voyage on 27 May 1936. Although of incomparable grandeur amongst British ships, she did not achieve her French rival's reputation for stability. The *Normandie* was built at the same time and was better able to maintain schedule in rough weather, the *Queen Mary* having to reduce speed to lessen the roll.
Radio Times Hulton Picture Library

Above: One of the dining rooms on the *Queen Mary* in 1936. A light on the map marked the ship's position. The provisioning necessary to feed thousands for five days was prodigious, entailing the carriage of at least 4,000 chickens, 100 sheep, 145 lambs, 16,000lb fish, 4,000 oysters, and 60,000 eggs. She had only three years of service before being painted grey and converted to a troopship in 1939. As she crossed the Atlantic 86 times and carried almost two million soldiers, it was considered a miracle that the *Queen Mary* did not meet with any danger, except in a collision with a British cruiser which sank. Until 1942, she had no radar, only two small guns and her speed precluded the possibility of escort.
Radio Times Hulton Picture Library

Centre left: A first class suite on the *Queen Mary* in May 1936. The panelling is walnut, perhaps the most fashionable wood in the 1930s. Doubtless the exposed fluorescent tubes were considered the last word in lighting — now they would be thought rather vulgar. The sprinkler system is also noteworthy.
Radio Times Hulton Picture Library

Left: On 12 August 1939, three weeks before her last prewar crossing, a Tourist class Gala Night is held aboard the *Queen Mary*. These were for tourist and third class passengers only, first class clientele being considered too sophisticated for such frivolities.
Radio Times Hulton Picture Library

Top: The *Ile de France* (43,450 tons) made her maiden voyage in June 1927. In the quest for having the 'largest' something, the bar on the *Ile de France* was the longest on the Atlantic — 27 feet. She became one of the most popular of all trans-Atlantic liners although she possessed certain undesirable or strange characteristics such as veneered panelling in the cabins which creaked whatever the weather or a bathroom weirdly decorated with monkeys rather than the more customary birds. After spending the war carrying troops, the *Ile de France* was refitted with two rather than three funnels but came to an ignominious end in the early sixties. The Japanese bought her for scrap and were exceptionally respectful in their feelings for the French when they took over the ship, but then allowed MGM to blow her up for a film *'The Last Voyage'*.
Radio Times Hulton Picture Library

Above: The SS *Normandie* (83,400 tons) was arguably the most impressively decorated liner ever built. Travellers seemed to love or loathe her, depending upon their feelings about gold, Lalique glass, scarlet and Le Corbusier whose influence or ideas seemed to be behind the startling concoction. Her maiden voyage began at Le Havre on 29 May 1935 with the wife of the President of the Republic, Madame Lebrun, in the main suite. The objective of taking the Blue Riband was achieved without difficulty and retained until the *Queen Mary* captured it in the following year. Tragedy struck in February 1942 after American officials had seized her in Manhattan on the fall of France. Foolishness was responsible for a fire in the grand salon and incompetence caused 3,500 tons of water to be poured into her which then froze and capsized her. Her dismissed French crew, cognisant of safety regulations and fire drill, might have prevented or contained the fire. She was sold for scrap.
Radio Times Hulton Picture Library

Below: The 40,000-ton *Bremen* was built for North German Lloyd and launched in August 1928. On her maiden voyage in July 1929, she took the Blue Riband but North German Lloyd found custom hard to win, however fast their flagship. Animosity towards Germany had not disappeared after the war and Hitler revived such feelings. One of the more unusual features of the *Bremen* was a shooting gallery in which film of game was projected until successfully shot. The film stopped and the point of the bullet's entry lit up so that the accuracy of the shot could be judged. The *Bremen* is seen here in dry dock at Southampton having her hull painted.
Radio Times Hulton Picture Library

Left: The *Deutschland* was the only really fast ship built for the Hamburg-Amerika line. After a brief spate of holding the laurels, the company conceded supremacy of speed to North German Lloyd. The vessel was heavy on coal but not as hungry as the *Mauretania* which bettered the *Deutschland*'s average speed by four knots. A game of shuffle-board is played on the sun deck of the *Deutschland*.   *F. S. Lincoln, Paul Popper*

Top: The shape of cross-channel ferries in the 1930s. *Queen of the Channel* was built by W. Denny & Bros of Dumbarton and entered service in 1935. Carrying nearly 1,500 passengers at 19 knots, she was owned by the London and Southend Continental Ship Company and managed by the New Medway Steam Packet Company. Her two diesel engines produced 3,000hp and the ship weighed 1,160 tons. *Radio Times Hulton Picture Library*

Above: The *Ich Dien* was owned by the Aberdeen Steamship Co and was the largest passenger-carrying tug on the Thames. She is seen here taking passengers to Tower Pier. *C. R. L. Coles/Ian Allan Library*

Above: Holyhead was the port for the Irish Mails even before the advent of railways. Telford had been employed improving what became the A5 and constructing his magnificent bridge over the Menai Straits. The construction of the Chester and Holyhead Railway, absorbed by the London and North Western Railway, ended the Irish mail coaches which had been amongst the fastest in the country. This shows the facilities created at Holyhead for the ferries to Dun Laoghaire for Dublin with *SS Cambria* on the right.
Ian Allan Library

Below: The promenade and Victoria pier at Douglas on the Isle of Man. As the name suggests, the island became a fashionable venue for day and holiday visitors, mostly sailing from Liverpool. Some of the vessels were owned by the London and North Western and later London Midland and Scottish Railway. The island railways were independently owned, however. The horse-tram along the promenade may be seen on the right.   *Ian Allan Library*